## WILDLIFE VIEWING AREAS

BAY OF BENGAL

New Delhi
Mumbai
Chennai

1. Bandipur National Park
2. Ranthambore National Park
3. Gir National Park
4. Little Rann of Kutch
5. Kaziranga National Park
6. Corbett National Park
7. Kanha National Park
8. Pench National Park
9. Bhitarkanika Mangroves
10. Sundarbans National Park
11. Periyar National Park & Wildlife Sanctuary
12. Dudhwa National Park
13. Dachigam National Park
14. Valmiki Wildlife Sanctuary
15. Manas National Park
16. Sariska National Park
17. Bandhavgarh National Park
18. Nagarhole National Park
19. Kanger Ghati National Park
20. Tadoba National Park
21. Indravati National Park
22. Kumarakom Bird Sanctuary
23. Parambikulam Wildlife Sanctuary
24. Gulf of Mannar Marine National Park

WILDLIFE SOS
INDIA

Researched by Wildlife SOS India. Illustrations show the adult male in breeding coloration unless stated otherwise. Measurements refer to maximum length of species from nose to tail tip. 'H'= shoulder height. Butterfly measurements denote wingspan.

Waterford Press produces reference guides that introduce novices to nature, science, travel and languages. Product information is featured on the website: www.waterfordpress.com

Text and illustrations © 2015, 2017 by Waterford Press Inc. All rights reserved. Cover images © Shutterstock.
To order, call 800-434-2555. For permissions, or to share comments, e-mail editor@waterfordpress.com
For information on custom-published products, call 800-434-2555 or e-mail info@waterfordpress.com

978-1-58355-940-6   $7.95
610315

Scan for more info

Made in the USA

---

# INDIA WILDLIFE

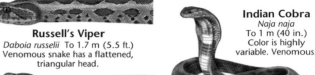

## A Folding Pocket Guide to Familiar Animals

INDIA WILDLIFE – A Folding Pocket Guide to Familiar Animals    Kavanagh/Leung

---

## BUTTERFLIES

**Painted Lady**
*Vanessa cardui*
To 6 cm (2.5 in.)
Tip of forewing is dark with white spots.

**Striped Tiger**
*Danaus genutia*
To 10 cm (4 in.)
One of India's most common butterflies.

**Plain Tiger**
*Danaus chrysippus*
To 8 cm (3 in.)

**Common Lascar**
*Pantoporia hordonia*
To 5 cm (2 in.)

**Blue Tiger**
*Tirumala limniace*
To 10 cm (4 in.)

**Leopard Lacewing**
*Cethosia cyane*
To 8 cm (3 in.)

**White Commodore**
*Parasarpa dudu*
To 9 cm (3.5 in.)

**Great Eggfly**
*Hypolimnas bolina*
To 9 cm (3.5 in.)

**Blue Pansy**
*Precis orithya*
To 5 cm (2 in.)

**Common Lime Butterfly**
*Papilio demoleus*
To 10 cm (4 in.)

**Red Pierrot**
*Talicada nyseus*
To 9 cm (3.5 in.)

**Common Banded Peacock**
*Papilio crino*
To 10 cm (4 in.)

**Dark Judy**
*Abisara fylla*
To 6 cm (2.5 in.)

**African Babul Blue**
*Azanus jezous*
To 3 cm (1 in.)

Underwings
**Common Jezebel**
*Delias eucharis*
To 9 cm (3.5 in.)

---

## REPTILES & AMPHIBIANS

**Common Indian Tree Frog**
*Polypedates maculatus*
To 8 cm (3 in.)
Color ranges from brown to whitish. Note yellow spots on thigh.

**Indian Green Frog**
*Euphlyctis hexadactylus*
To 13 cm (5 in.)

**Common Asian Toad**
*Duttaphrynus melanostictus*
To 20 cm (8 in.)

**Common Garden Lizard**
*Calotes versicolor*
To 38 cm (15 in.)
Note spikey crest on head and neck.

**Termite Hill Gecko**
*Hemidactylus triedrus*
To 20 cm (8 in.)
Color ranges from black-grey to pinkish-brown.

**Brahminy Skink**
*Eutropis carinata*
To 33 cm (13 in.)

**Gliding Lizard**
*Draco dussumieri* To 23 cm. (9 in.)
Capable of gliding between trees for distances up to 60 m (200 ft.).

**Indian Star Tortoise**
*Geochelone elegans*
To 25 cm (10 in.)

**Indian Chameleon**
*Chamaeleo zeylanicus*
To 38 cm (15 in.)

**Common Indian Monitor**
*Varanus bengalensis*
To 1.8 m (6 ft.)

**Green Vine Snake**
*Ahaetulla nasuta* To 2 m (6.5 ft.)
Slender snake has a pointed nose.

**Indian Python**
*Python molurus* To 3 m (10 ft.)

**Banded Sea Krait**
*Laticauda colubrina*
To 1.4 m (56 in.)
Venomous.

**Common Indian Krait**
*Bungarus fasciatus*
To 2.1 m (7 ft.)
Venomous.

---

## REPTILES & AMPHIBIANS

**Russell's Viper**
*Daboia russelii* To 1.7 m (5.5 ft.)
Venomous snake has a flattened, triangular head.

**Indian Cobra**
*Naja naja*
To 1 m (40 in.)
Color is highly variable. Venomous.

**Saw-scaled Viper**
*Echis carinatus* To 60 cm (2 ft.)
When threatened, it inflates its body and rubs its scales together to create a hissing sound. Venomous.

**Mugger Crocodile**
*Crocodylus palustris* To 4.5 m (15 ft.)
Also called the marsh crocodile.

**King Cobra**
*Ophiophagus hannah*
To 5.7 m (19 ft.)
Color ranges from greenish to black. Note light yellow crossbands along body. The largest venomous snake in the world.

**Gharial**
*Gavialis gangeticus* To 6 m (20 ft.)
Slender snout has 110 teeth. Feeds primarily on fish.

## BIRDS

**Little Grebe**
*Tachybaptus ruficollis*
To 30 cm (12 in.)
Also called dabchick.

**Knob-billed Duck**
*Sarkidiornis melanotos*
To 75 cm (30 in.)
Also called comb duck.

**Eurasian Coot**
*Fulica atra*
To 40 cm (16 in.)

**Little Cormorant**
*Microcarbo niger*
To 50 cm (20 in.)

**Black-headed Gull**
*Chroicocephalus ridibundus*
To 38 cm (15 in.)

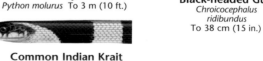

**Indian Darter**
*Anhinga melanogaster*
To 1 m (40 in.)

---

## BIRDS

**Cattle Egret**
*Bubulcus ibis*
To 50 cm (20 in.)

**Great Egret**
*Ardea alba* To 95 cm (38 in.)
Note yellow bill and black feet.

**Little Egret**
*Egretta garzetta*
To 65 cm (26 in.)
Note black bill and yellow feet.

**Eurasian Spoonbill**
*Platalea leucorodia*
To 90 cm (3 ft.)
Bill has a spoon-shaped tip.

**White Stork**
*Ciconia ciconia*
To 1.2 m (4 ft.)

**Indian Pond Heron**
*Ardeola grayii*
To 45 cm (18 in.)

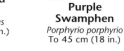

**Little Heron**
*Butorides striatus*
To 35 cm (14 in.)
Note black cap.

**Red-wattled Lapwing**
*Vanellus indicus*
To 35 cm (14 in.)
Red bill has a black tip.

**Purple Swamphen**
*Porphyrio porphyrio*
To 45 cm (18 in.)

**Grey Heron**
*Ardea cinerea*
To 95 cm (38 in.)

**Common Kingfisher**
*Alcedo atthis*
To 18 cm (7 in.)

**White-throated Kingfisher**
*Halcyon smyrnensis*
To 28 cm (11 in.)

**Spotted Dove**
*Spilopelia chinensis*
To 33 cm (13 in.)
Note white-spotted
black collar on neck.

**Rock Pigeon**
*Columba livia*
To 33 cm (13 in.)

**Laughing Dove**
*Spilopelia senegalensis*
To 25 cm (10 in.)
Note spots on neck.

**Asian Koel**
*Eudynamys scolopaceus*
To 45 cm (18 in.)
Note red eyes.

**Green Bee-eater**
*Merops orientalis*
To 18 cm (7 in.)

**Indian Vulture**
*Gyps indicus*
To 1 m (40 in.)

**Greater Coucal**
*Centropus sinensis*
To 48 cm (19 in.)

**Coppersmith Barbet**
*Megalaima haemacephala*
To 18 cm (7 in.)
Repetitive call – tuk-tuk-tuk –
has been likened to a
hammer striking metal.

**Black Kite**
*Milvus migrans*
To 55 cm (22 in.)

**Large Green Barbet**
*Megalaima zeylanica*
To 28 cm (11 in.)

**Purple Sunbird**
*Nectarinia asiatica*
To 10 cm (4 in.)

**Indian Peafowl**
*Pavo cristatus*
To 2 m (80 in.)
National bird of India.

**Indian Roller**
*Coracias benghalensis*
To 28 cm (11 in.)

**Common Myna**
*Acridotheres tristis*
To 23 cm (9 in.)

**Oriental Magpie-Robin**
*Copsychus saularis*
To 19 cm (7.5 in.)

**Red-vented Bulbul**
*Pycnonotus cafer*
To 22 cm (8.5 in.)

**House Crow**
*Corvus splendens*
To 40 cm (16 in.)

**Common Tailorbird**
*Orthotomus sutorius*
To 14 cm (5.5 in.)
Familiar backyard species
'sews' together its nest of
leaves. Song is a loud
*cheeup-cheeup-cheeup.*

**Crested Hoopoe**
*Upupa epops*
To 30 cm (12 in.)
Head crest is erect when
alarmed. Call is a soft
repeated – hoop-hoop.

**Plum-headed Parakeet**
*Psittacula cyanocephala*
To 35 cm (14 in.)

**Rose-ringed Parakeet**
*Psittacula krameri*
To 40 cm (16 in.)
Male has black
chin stripe and
pink collar.

**Indian Grey Hornbill**
*Ocyceros birostris*
To 60 cm (2 ft.)

**Great Hornbill**
*Buceros bicornis*
To 1.1 m (44 in.)

**Black Drongo**
*Dicrurus macrocercus*
To 28 cm (11 in.)
Note white spot
near beak.

**House Sparrow**
*Passer domesticus*
To 15 cm (6 in.)

**Black-naped Blue Monarch**
*Hypothymis azurea*
To 15 cm (6 in.)

**Indian Pangolin**
*Manis crassicaudata*
To 1.2 m (4 ft.)
Body is covered with
heavy scales. Rolls into
a ball when threatened.
Eats ants and termites.
Endangered.

**Indian Hare**
*Lepus nigricollis*
To 70 cm (28 in.)
Note dark patch on
neck. Also called
black-naped hare.

**Indian Flying Fox**
*Pteropus giganteus*
To 40 cm (16 in.)
Nocturnal species
feeds primarily on
fruit.

**Indian Hedgehog**
*Paraechinus micropus*
To 28 cm (11 in.)

**Indian Palm Squirrel**
*Funambulus palmarum*
To 20 cm (8 in.)

**Small Indian Mongoose**
*Herpestes javanicus*
To 65 cm (26 in.)

**Indian Giant Squirrel**
*Ratufa indica*
To 90 cm (3 ft.)
Color ranges from tan to
dark brown. Underparts are
cream-colored.

**Indian Grey Mongoose**
*Herpestes edwardsi*
To 90 cm (3 ft.)

**Honey Badger (Ratel)**
*Mellivora capensis*
To 75 cm (30 in.)

**Smooth Coated Otter**
*Lutrogale perspicillata*
To 1 m (40 in.)

**Small Indian Civet**
*Viverricula indica*
To 1 m (40 in.)

**Indian Crested Porcupine**
*Hystrix indica* To 1 m (40 in.)

**Red Panda**
*Ailurus fulgens* To 1.2 m (4 ft.)
The only living species of the
Family Ailuridae; it was
previously classified as both
a bear and a raccoon.

**Grey Langur**
*Semnopithecus entellus*
To 1.8 m (6 ft.)
Common near human settlements.
Also called Hanuman langur.
**National mammal of India.**

**Lion-tailed Macaque**
*Macaca silenus* To 75 cm (30 in.)
Endangered.

**Bonnet Macaque**
*Macaca radiata*
To 1.2 m (4 ft.)
Endemic to southern
India, it is common near
human settlements.

**Golden Jackal**
*Canis aureus* To 1 m (40 in.)
Note dark tip on tail.

**Rhesus Macaque**
*Macaca mulatta*
To 75 cm (30 in.)
Common near
human
settlements.

**Dhole**
*Cuon alpinus* To 1.5 m (5 ft.)
Also called Indian wild dog.
Endangered.

**Bengal Fox**
*Vulpes bengalensis* To 70 cm (28 in.)
Endemic species. Also called
Indian fox.

**Indian Boar**
*Sus scrofa cristatus*
To 1.5 m (5 ft.)
Note back bristles.

**Sloth Bear**
*Melursus ursinus* To 1.8 m (6 ft.)
Has a long, shaggy coat, pale
muzzle and white claws. Feeds
primarily on ants and termites.

**Asiatic Black Bear**
*Ursus thibetanus* To 1.8 m (6 ft.)
Feeds on plants and animals as
big as a water buffalo. Also
called moon bear for its
'U'-shaped chest patch.

**Striped Hyena**
*Hyaena hyaena* To 1.7 m (5.5 ft.)
Note shaggy coat and prominent mane.

**Caracal**
*Caracal caracal* To 45 cm (18 in.) H
Note large, tasseled ears.
Found in NW India.

**Indian Leopard**
*Panthera pardus fusca*
To 2.3 m (7.5 ft.)

**Indian Lion**
*Panthera leo persica* To 3 m (10 ft.)
Found only in Gir National Park.
Endangered.

**Bengal Tiger**
*Panthera tigris tigris*
To 3.6 m (12 ft.)
**National animal of
India.** Endangered.

**Jungle Cat**
*Felis chaus* To 1.3 m (52 in.)
Note tufted ears.

**Snow Leopard**
*Panthera uncia*
To 2.3 m (7.5 ft.)
Endangered
Himalayan wild cat.

**Barking Deer**
*Muntiacus muntjak*
To 53 cm (21 in.)
Also called Indian muntjac,
it makes a bark-like call
upon spotting a predator.

**Sambar Deer**
*Rusa unicolor* To 3 m (10 ft.)
Huge deer has a shaggy coat.
Males have large, forked antlers.

**Siberian Ibex**
*Capra sibirica* To 1.1 m (44 in.) H
Males have curved, ridged horns
to 4 ft. (1.2 m) long.

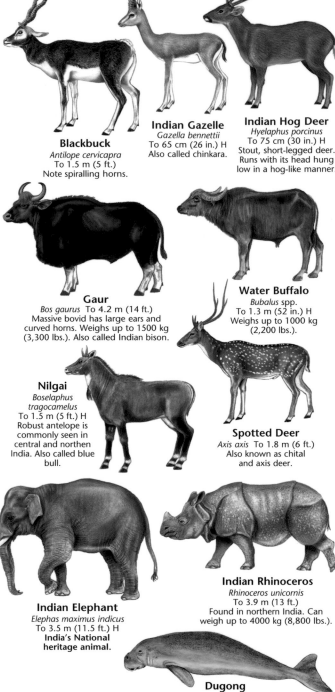
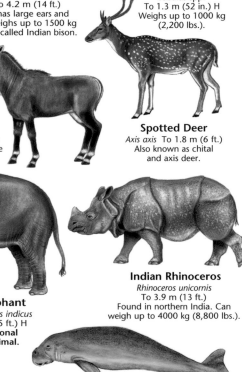

**Blackbuck**
*Antilope cervicapra*
To 1.5 m (5 ft.)
Note spiralling horns.

**Indian Gazelle**
*Gazella bennettii*
To 65 cm (26 in.) H
Also called chinkara.

**Indian Hog Deer**
*Hyelaphus porcinus*
To 75 cm (30 in.) H
Stout, short-legged deer.
Runs with its head hung
low in a hog-like manner.

**Gaur**
*Bos gaurus* To 4.2 m (14 ft.)
Massive bovid has large ears and
curved horns. Weighs up to 1500 kg
(3,300 lbs.). Also called Indian bison.

**Water Buffalo**
*Bubalus* spp.
To 1.3 m (52 in.) H
Weighs up to 1000 kg
(2,200 lbs.).

**Nilgai**
*Boselaphus tragocamelus*
To 1.5 m (5 ft.) H
Robust antelope is
commonly seen in
central and northern
India. Also called blue
bull.

**Spotted Deer**
*Axis axis* To 1.8 m (6 ft.)
Also known as chital
and axis deer.

**Indian Elephant**
*Elephas maximus indicus*
To 3.5 m (11.5 ft.) H
India's National
heritage animal.

**Indian Rhinoceros**
*Rhinoceros unicornis*
To 3.9 m (13 ft.)
Found in northern India. Can
weigh up to 4000 kg (8,800 lbs.).

**Dugong**
*Dugong dugon* To 3.3 m (11 ft.)
Lives in shallow coastal waters